I AM SCHIZOPHRENIC

Poetry From A Beautiful Brain

KERENZA RYAN

Printed by Amazon, in the United States of America.

ISBN: 9781099248382

Cover Designed by Autumn Wolf.

First Printing, 2019.

www.kerenzaryan.com

To all the people who helped me through my illness.
I wish all of you knew who you are.
If you're not sure, this includes you.

TABLE OF CONTENTS

PREFACE

This book started in a lot of different points. You could say it started at 16 when I was both first published and first suicidal. You could say it started at 19 when I was first delusional. You could say it started at 20 when I was first hospitalized and diagnosed, or at 21 when I did a senior seminar project where I wrote and presented a collection of mental health poetry. Any of these answers are fine, but I see this as a lifetime work. All my experiences affect all my other experiences, because that's how memory works.

That's also how mental illness works. My delusions (beliefs that aren't true like 'the world is a simulation') often relate to my hallucinations (sights, sounds, smells, tastes, touches, etc. that aren't real). My depression sometimes causes panic attacks. My lack of interest in everyday activities can cause oversleeping or eating. I've been doing much better recently, in that I've been getting better and better over the last few years. But I still have symptoms, and I probably always will. Understanding this will make a big difference in understanding my poetry.

There was a time when I thought I would take medication and everything would go away. In that case why spend time and money writing about it? Since that is not the case, I strive to be understood. I want people to know about my life, so I feel less alone. And hopefully, other people who struggle with mental illness, or just struggle in general, will feel less alone as well.

My Brain is Beautiful

Sometimes my brain
Works against me
It creates scary thing
That are not there
But other times
It creates Poetry

In the Imagination
Both are beautiful

Diagnosis

Names change
From one doctor to the next
"Not an exact science"
Sometimes it feels
Like it's not a science at all
But the hard word
That always sticks around
Is psychosis

Names

Panic disorder is clear
      (I panic)
But if one more person
Asks what schizoaffective depression is...

      (I'll probably panic)

Mental Health Days

Curl up with a journal

Write out delusion after delusion

Text a friend

Run from the demon

Hide from the camera

Overeat or don't eat at all

Take sleeping medication till the next day comes

Smile! You're on Camera

A camera is following me
Just behind my head
It can read my thoughts
It's recording everything
I'm being judged

I Don't Drink Whiskey

I don't drink whisky
But I drink in thunder
On the days when air becomes rain
And the yellow street lights
Turn the world into an old movie

I drink in thunder
Till nothing is real
And the camera through which I look at the world
Shakes and sways

I run along roads in the rainy dark
In the thunder
And contemplate jumping in front of cars
Not to feel something
(Cold rain guarantees that
Soaking through my shirt
For the men sitting under the awning
To whistle at)
But to see if perhaps
The world is as unreal as it seems

I run till I am tired and lost
I consider calling you
Calling anyone
To help me find my way back
But it's still raining

And you're not real either
Even if you say my name
Interact with me
And don't know how to deal with my
Crap

It might pull me out of it
Forced social interaction
But it's uncomfortable
To force myself into an unreal world
Entirely different from reading, reading, reading, reading a novel
And I'm not sure I want to be in the real world
So mental health be damned
I walk back in the rain
Not really feeling the slosh of water
From cars So Close
And when I wander around enough
I come to a sign I recognize
A shining green clue
I wonder who gifted me with it

The thought terrifies me
Noises too loud
Colors too bright
The world, too chaotic to be real
I run again with my terror energy
Fumble with and drop, drop, drop my keys
Break into an apartment
I can't be sure is mine

Anything could be reality
The corners of rooms seem flat
A cube drawn on rough brown paper
I can't be sure what's behind those corners
Doors could open to anything
I'm too scared to shower

Instead I put a blanket over my head
Shiver in the wet warmth
My fear doesn't end with hiding
So I put on an old detective show
And watch, rewatch, rewatch, rewatch,
Meant to be unreal
Always wrapped up in an hour
And more familiar than my bedroom

I can never shut out all the noise though
Even as I buy headphones again again again
So I drink in the thunder
And wish I drank whisky

Thought Blocking

My mind stutters
Can't come up with the thoughts
A skipping record
You wait patiently through the "um"s and "uh"s
But no thoughts come

Hunting

I wish I could hunt out my sorrow
Shoot out the tiny pieces of me that hate myself
That want to lay in bed all day
But it's one thing to take out soldiers
And another to take out yourself

Breathless

Sometimes,
     I feel like I can't breathe
Sometimes,
     it's the tightening in my chest
Sometimes,
     it's the room's small space
Sometimes,
     words repeat in my head
Sometimes,
     (preservation)
Sometimes.
     what's the point of breathing anyway?

On My Medicine

Dust mites cloud my brain
Settling in the crevices
Rendering connections slow.
I used to long for speed,
But now my fumbling, grimy thoughts
Are Comforting.

Band-Aid

They say to rip it off fast
One smooth motion
The flood of pain meant to drown

Sometimes though
A steady hand
      (not my own)
Requires it to be ripped off
bit by bit by bit…

The skin prunes, unused
The scab prickles, polkadotting with blood,
The stretch of a finger tears
It open again

Another Band-aid
Another day

The skin grows into a scar
Inside a hand-me-down Band-aid
Not overnight
      (like I had hoped)
bit by bit by bit…

<u>Nothing</u>

Ever since,
As a young child,
A science museum displayed a vacuum to my brother and I
I have obsessed over the Possibility of
A Nothing.

But we got older
And gaining belief can lead
To more hallowed eyes
Than starry.

He tried to fill it up
With needles, knives, and women
And I let air and soul leak out
Too thin to fill a room or corpse
With anything but haze.

But I later learned of outer space:
A vacuum
A Nothing
Filled to the bursting point, constantly expanding
Arteries of light streaming through the air
Beat forward by a thousand suns
Gyres swirling ever out into infinity
Black holes and mistakes
Not redacting the chaos of the color
But admitting the power of autocannibalism

And leaping life forward anyway

Ever since
I've wanted to go back to the museum
And let Everything into the vacuum
Because it's most important to Learn that

A Nothing
Can hold
A Something
Once again.

Ceramics

A gentle pressure with the foot
The wheel turns, turns, turns
Rhythmic. Smooth.
The clay forms slow. Constant.
"Shit!"
Lined hands pull it off-kilter
The walls are too thin
The base is too heavy
It is wrong.
Perhaps the metaphor lies
In a life unaided by others
But God,
I can't help questioning
If your hands are skilled

Tomorrow Never Dies

Often, psychosis gets better around age forty.
Why?
No one knows
I don't know many teenagers looking forward
To their latter years
And I don't know if I am either
But it gives me a reason to live on
Just like tomorrow
I hope to never die
(Which may be an improvement)

She's Going the Distance

Vulnerability requires
A bit of courage
A dash of hope
And a whole lot of ego

I understand why it's a compliment,
But I don't think
People see the real me

The Monster of Me

The monster overtaking me
Must be showing through
I don't know how your eyes
Can handle looking to
My disfigured body
A mirror of my soul
I've always wanted morals
But don't know where to go.

You make me feel this way,
Won't look hear see touch know,
If I'm worth noticing,
It doesn't really show.

I know it's partly my fault,
The way I look and way I sound,
But actions are for reasoning,
Not just for shoving down.

The monster overtaking me
A mirror of my soul
If I am worth noticing
It does not really show.

Faking It

There's a demon following me
There's something evil in my stomach
I can read people's minds
I'd feel better if I jumped in front of a car
I'm invincible
The world is a simulation
Good, how are you?

Untitled

Anonymous

I lay in my bed in the morning, not wanting to get up,
Most teenagers don't want to get up.
But then I do, rolling out of bed which rips the covers off of it and
cocoons me in them,
For just a moment.
I bask in the feeling.

Then I pull them off of me and waddle into the bathroom,
And begin pulling at the knot that is my hair.
I must fix it, ugly is noticeable,
So is beauty.
Today I will blow dry,
But not straighten.

I think about makeup, looking at it with reverence, but then I put it
away again.
I have the time, but not the effort.
Not the effort to be noticed.
I slip back into my bedroom, and almost shut the door,
Leave the crack that makes most pause before entering.
I don't want to be closed,
But you're most definitely not invited in.

I look through clothes, pull on jeans, begin to open the shirt drawer.
I pull out a bright shirt, slim, pretty.

I slip it on, look in the mirror.
Today, I will be beautiful.
I slip a dark hoodie over it.

I grab my backpack, full of half-done homework,
And no doodles.
I tread lightly down the stairs, and grab a banana for breakfast.
I must eat something, not be too skinny, and though I'm not yet hungry,
Eating food during class makes noise.

I slip on my shoes before walking to the bus stop,
Plain, black and white, but low grade name brand.
Just enough.
I wish for a coat, a cocoon, but I will only be alone for a second.
I get there when the bus does, and slip in the upper middle.
I rest my eyes, and lean against my blue backpack, but do not sleep,
What if I snored?

I get to school, and get out, middle of the line.
Here my job becomes hard.
I open the door for myself, and hold it just long enough for the next person to grab it,
Being neither mean nor courteous.

First I walk around with my backpack on,
(No one's taken out their books yet)
And do a circle about three times.
Exactly three times.

It takes exactly three minutes.
If I go for too much longer, people will begin to notice.
I change my circle.

Finally the time comes,
And I am able to go up to my locker in peace.
I walk up the stairs, not using my normal fast footfall,
But staying exactly a foot from the person in front of me.
I go to my locker, and stand by the crowd blocking my way, against a
wall,
Until they decide to move.

I work to open my locker while keeping my backpack out of the new
crowd's way,
But I miss the next number in the combination.
I am focusing too much to focus.
I want to scream in anger, to kick it,
But instead I fumble for the first number again.
Then I take out my books.

I realize I fumbled on purpose, trying to take up time,
And wish I would've done it again.
Five more minutes till my classroom time.
I walk down the stairs, books clutched to my chest,
Both arms.
It shows self consciousness, and I try to shift it to the right like most
kids,
But I am left handed and see that this will not work.
I decide to stay in the middle.

At first I looked at my feet, or at the wall,
But now I know better.
Straight ahead, slight angle down, blank stare.
Let your eyes unfocus, really.

I walk to the library.
I think about going to the cafeteria, the hub of the people,
But someone may reach for me in the crowd.

I go straight to the computers, not a big table all alone,
And log on.
I have nothing to do this morning but not to be killed by time,
So I open up too many windows, and take my time closing them.
I wonder if anyone notices I'm doing nothing.
No one does.
I look at the clock again, two minutes to five minutes.
I log off.

I walk back up the stairs, head angled, books set,
But I realize I am here too early.
I do another circle, and finally 'five minutes till' comes.
I rush back to my classroom, hoping today it will not be locked.
I see with relief that I am spared.

I sit in a corner in the back, outside of the view of the door.
I am the first one here, but I do not mind that.
It is not too early when someone else comes in.
I pull out my pre-determined half finished math homework.
I have only come in early to finish, of course.
Of course.

Footsteps come close, and I rush to get a book out.

People will interrupt homework, but not a book.

This is not a good long term goal, a book every morning,

Because other people read.

Plus someone may notice the book never changes.

So, when the footsteps pass my room, rushing to someplace else, I put it away again.

Today I will have to pass for pleasantries.

It is a monday, maybe I will not even have to give them.

Two people come in as a group,

And are talking to each other with some excitement, so I am safe.

Slowly more and more people, weave in the room.

Before class starts, and I begin focusing too much to focus again,

I allow one more coherent thought:

It's too early for fake in the morning.

Knowing full well I will repeat it to myself throughout the day,

When trying to slip out of a bustling cafeteria with a much needed lunch,

But eventually settling to not eat for hours,

And again when going home

To spend the rest of Friday afternoon and evening and night in my bed,

cocooned in the sheets.

It's too early for fake in the morning.

Oven

Some days I dream about sticking my head in an oven
It stopped scaring me a while ago
I don't know if I'd ever do it
But I find the thought comforting.

Night Terrors

I have night terrors
Awake and fully functioning
At night I am hunted
At night I am weak
I pray for protection
I am still alive
Night after Night
So renewed terror means that You heard me

I

Demons overflood my house
Fill every nook and cranny
I can feel them pressing in on all sides
This place is holy evil
And so am I.

Dinner Blessings

My prayers drip mental illness
A wretched spirit and a broken mind
I don't know if you can hear
Through the stutter
I don't know if I have anything to say

help.

Jealous Love

Psychosis is my best friend
Always present
Whispering in my ear
Shaping my worldview
Overtaking other friendships
But it never listens

Punching a Wall

Bloodied knuckles
And blue bruises
Brick walls
In hallowed halls
Unhealthy coping
Fatigued fingers

A Good Night's Sleep

Everyone says they're always tired

As if it's an emotion

Perhaps it overtakes emotions

Swallows up thoughts

Clouds over morals

Maybe if we just got a good night's sleep we'd know

Jump

I wanted to jump off a bridge
Into the rushing water below
To put out the electricity in my body
And finally be human

My Heart Is Not My Own

I open up to strangers
Pull out my heart
And watch it beat in their hands

Contradiction

I can read people's thoughts
But can't guess what they're going to say
It's a contradiction
But I live in it

Simulation

The world is a trick
Played by God
Completely unreal
But all I've ever known

Overstimulation

Noise overtakes me
Concentration is a feat too great for me
Colors are brighter, more vibrant
blinding
Every cell of my skin feels the air
I close my eyes and roll up
The only thing I can't feel is You there

Dead Grace

Sometimes I believe
That one day life will be different
Just because I woke up that way

I watch comets melt
Through the sky
Once a year or a decade or a millennia
Or just Once

And I wonder if I'm waiting
For a Just Once

Like the seed on the big
Brown maple tree out back
That only need spin to the ground
Once
To be planted
And grow taller than I ever could

Or the little infant
That comes out bloody and screaming
But comes out nonetheless
No political agenda necessary
Before, hidden, forming, connected
Suddenly
Itself

But I am not a comet
Or an infant
Or even a tree
Perhaps my grace already came
Because I'm alive
And I'm sober
And you're not

And perhaps it hasn't

Perhaps it never will

Perhaps I will be eaten up by the sun
Choked out by the weeds
Miscarried painfully
Dead on Arrival
Dead before Arrival
Dead.

And the bug that really gnaws away at my roots
Is that I'll just never know

Better

I worry when I'm doing better
That I'll get worse again

And that I won't

Life is Better Healthy

A classmate once asked
About writing during An Episode

(It's big and ineligible
It's ranting and scared)
      (I hope it's not me)

When will people believe
Life is Better healthy?

"You Have Schizophrenia"

I am schizophrenic
Mental Health Officials
Rant and rave
Over me defining myself
With something
That is not a character flaw

Schizoaffective Fear

I'm afraid I'll want to hurt others
That a delusion will overtake me so completely
That I'm unsafe
I can't negate the possibility

Slurred Words

I want to grip and shake you
Tell you "crazy" is a slur
But then you'd just turn it on me

Now

Home is where the mind is
Where I can unload delusions
Take antipsychotics
And feel myself
I haven't found home quite yet

A Beautiful Brain

Am I interesting
Simply because my mind works differently than others
Because you can ask me
About my scariest hallucinations
And I can tell you
About the bugs in my eyes
And the hand around my throat
I've always longed to be interesting
Now I'm not sure I'm ready to pay the price

Made in the USA
Middletown, DE
14 May 2024

54231137R00033